GOOD GIRL GLADY

MANDY POTTER

ILLUSTRATED BY WENNY STEFANIE

Copyright © 2023. All rights reserved. This book or parts thereof may not be reproduced in any form, stored in any retrieval system, or transmitted in any form by any means- electronic, mechanical, photocopy, recording or otherwise- without prior written permission of the publisher, except as provided by the Canadian copyright law.

This book is dedicated to the dog who inspired it, Gladys (Glady) Angel Eye Potter. It's also dedicated to the white poodles that came before her, Jazzy and Brandy. And lastly, to Joey Potter, the best dog mom and grand*paw*rent in the world.

This book is also dedicated to the countless and selfless individuals who foster, adopt, and save senior animals.

Drawings by Division 5, Grade 4 and 5 students at šxʷwəq̓ʷəθət Crosstown Elementary

Long ago, I was a tiny puppy that my family adored. But over time, I grew old, and so did they. By the time I was 16 years old, their lives had gotten so busy that they forgot about me. I became sad and lonely.

I always heard other people say "good girl" or "good boy" to their dogs. I never heard anyone say, "Good girl, Glady."

I decided that if they didn't need me, then I didn't need them! I would leave and find a new family and home.

I couldn't walk anymore, but it wasn't long until some friendly people found me and wrapped me in a warm blanket. They even gave me a treat! I hadn't had one of those in years.

They called my family, but nobody came. A kind lady gave me medicine for my pain, and I heard them say that the doctor would fix my leg the next day.

However, my leg was hurt so badly that they had to remove it. But it was okay. My pain was gone, and I could walk around just fine with three legs. They put a funny cone on my head to stop me from licking the spot where my leg used to be. That was a good idea because it was so itchy!

After I had been at the shelter for a few weeks, I heard the shelter lady say that they had been trying to find me a new home, but they hadn't had any luck. I liked the shelter, but I was ready for a family to call my own.

People came to the shelter every day, but they walked right past my kennel. I kept seeing other dogs being adopted, and while I was so happy for my friends, I couldn't help but wish I was going home with a nice family too.

I heard one of the shelter ladies say to another that I hadn't been adopted yet because I was too old and only had three legs. That made me sad because I couldn't change those things. I hoped someone would adopt me soon and love me just the way I was.

Then, one day, a girl with tattoos stopped at my kennel door. At first, I thought she would keep walking as everyone else had. But she looked at me in awe, like she had seen someone famous. The door opened, and she gave me a big hug.

She walked me to the front desk, and the shelter ladies gave me big hugs too. It was finally my turn to be adopted!

My new mom said, "You don't belong here. You're coming home with me. You're such a good girl, Glady."
I was over the moon!

When we got home, I met my other new mom, my two dog sisters named Billy and Iggy, and a human baby sister named Beau. *Wow! A big family just for me!* I thought.

My family went everywhere together: on planes to places I had never seen before,

and to the mall in my special bag.

We had a big yard where I felt like a puppy again and could run around. I loved going there. It quickly became my favourite place in the world.

The days turned to weeks, weeks to months, and months to years. We spent our days together, and I felt so much love.

As time passed, I began to get even older and more tired. Eventually, I lost my eyesight and hearing.

One day, I heard my family say it was getting close to being "my time." I agreed. I had such a good life, but I was 21 years old. I was tired, and my bones ached. I didn't even want my favourite foods anymore.

To celebrate my life, my family had a special dinner for me with Grandma, Grandpa, and our best friends. Everyone was petting me and saying, "Good girl, Glady." Then, when it was time for them to leave, they all gave me a long goodbye and a kiss on the forehead.

As I fell asleep, Mom kissed me and said, "You'll always be my good girl, Glady." Mom was so sad, but she didn't need to be. I knew we would see each other again someday.

I crossed the rainbow bridge and noticed I had all four legs again. I could even see and hear! I saw myself in a puddle, and I was a puppy again.

It was a beautiful place and looked a lot like the cabin. The weather was perfect, and I felt the wind in my fur as I sniffed the fresh mountain air. In the distance, I could see my family's dogs that had crossed the rainbow bridge before me. Before running over to greet them, I looked back to say a final goodbye to Mom.

I knew that I would forever be Good Girl Glady.

www.ingramcontent.com/pod-product-compliance
Lightning Source LLC
Chambersburg PA
CBHW051321110526
44590CB00031B/4429